Original title:
Candy Canes and Candlelight

Copyright © 2024 Creative Arts Management OÜ
All rights reserved.

Author: Levi Montgomery
ISBN HARDBACK: 978-9916-90-960-7
ISBN PAPERBACK: 978-9916-90-961-4

Sweet Echoes of a Winter's Night

Snowflakes dance like clumsy fools,
While children sled down icy pools.
Hot cocoa spills upon my knee,
As winter laughs and shouts with glee.

Frosty breath forms clouds of cheer,
While squirrels gear up with festive gear.
The snowman winks, his carrot nose,
Says he steals hearts, 'cause everyone knows.

Icicles hang like nature's bling,
Voices echo, let the laughter ring.
We slip and slide, a comedy show,
In winter's grasp, we steal the snow.

So here's to nights with frosty charms,
Chasing snowflakes in each other's arms.
With mittens lost and boots all wet,
Winter's wonders, we'll never forget.

The Magic in Twisted Sticks

In the forest, sticks and dreams collide,
The squirrels debate, with great pride.
One says, 'Twist it, toss it high!'
The other snickers, 'Watch it fly!'

They gather twigs that twist and twirl,
From tangled roots to the edge of a whirl.
The magic's real with every bend,
And every stick promises a new friend.

A crooked branch with a pointy cap,
Claims it's the best for a wizard's map.
It points to places where pinecones sing,
And the frogs drum beats in a woodland fling.

So grab your stick, let it cast a spell,
In this twisted world, we laugh and yell.
With sticks in hand, let's dance and prance,
In the magic of play, we all take a chance.

Sweetness Wrapped in Twinkling Moments

Candy clouds float in the air,
Gummy bears dance without a care.
Chocolate rivers, oh what a sight,
Sipping sweet tea under starlight.

Cupcakes giggle, icing's so bright,
Sprinkles rain down, what pure delight!
Pies doing cartwheels, a messy affair,
Life is sweeter when treats are there.

Radiant Reflections of a Cozy Night

Under a blanket, cuddled up tight,
Laughs echo softly, all feels right.
Popcorn pops with a cheerful sound,
Funny cat videos abound.

Mugs of hot cocoa, marshmallows afloat,
A dog snores loudly, dreams on a boat.
The moon winks down with a cheesy smile,
Let's cozy up and stay for a while.

The Lure of Sugary Shadows

In the kitchen, shadows dance near,
Whiskers of sugar draw us near.
Muffins whisper secrets of bliss,
Who can resist a sugary kiss?

Lollipops hiding like cheeky sprites,
Candy bars join in the silly fights.
Each bite's a giggle, each munch a song,
In sugary realms, we all belong.

Twisted Delights Under the Stars

Under the stars, the donuts twirl,
Fried treats jump and perform a whirl.
Brownies with wigs prance on the ground,
Laughter erupts, very unbound.

Cookies wear sunglasses, feeling so cool,
While cupcakes debate who's the biggest fool.
Soda pops fizz with a loud cheer,
Life is a circus when sweets are near.

Twinkling Treats of the Season

Twinkling lights on gingerbread,
Sugar plums dance in my head.
Cookies piled way too high,
Watch me eat – oh me, oh my!

Mistletoe sneaks up with cheer,
Kissing folks without a fear.
Frosting lands on my best hat,
I look like a very sweet cat!

Festive Whispers in the Dark

In the night, the whispers play,
Chocolate cakes on display.
Sounds of laughter, ringing bells,
Even my cat's under spells!

Every shadow hides a treat,
Gingerbread men try to cheat!
Elves on shelves, they watch in glee,
Plotting ways to tickle me!

Sugar-Streaked Radiance

Candy canes in every hue,
I might eat them all, it's true!
Sprinkles flying through the air,
Sweet chaos beyond compare!

Marshmallow snowballs, fluffy white,
Chasing friends with all my might.
Laughter echoes, joy prevails,
As we dance like crazy snails!

Flickering Flames and Frosted Dreams

Flickering flames, a cozy glow,
Building s'mores – oh what a show!
Stockings hung with socks so bold,
Filled with treats and stories told.

Snowflakes fall like sugary dust,
Giggling is a daily must.
Frosted windows, laughter flows,
Life's a party, that's how it goes!

Jingle of Sweets Beneath the Trees

In the kitchen, pots clang and clatter,
Cookies and cakes make the belly patter.
Flour on faces, a sprinkle of cheer,
Sweet tooth's laughter rings loud and clear.

The cat tries to sneak a delicious bite,
But we catch her just in time, what a sight!
Gingerbread men run, oh what a scene,
Frosting and candy, a sugary dream.

Twinkling Aromas in Frosty Air

The oven's on fire, oh what a smell,
Cinnamon rolls rise like a sweet little spell.
Hot cocoa fountains want to take a swim,
With marshmallows bobbing, it's joy on a whim.

Outside it is chilly, but we warm the heart,
With cookies and laughter, each part is a part.
Frost on the windows, but the kitchen's aglow,
Laughter and sweets, our own winter show.

Sweet Stripes of Winter's Glow

Candy canes twirl, oh what a delight,
Stripes of peppermint twinkling at night.
Elves in the corner, all giggles and grins,
Sneaking some treats, let the fun begin!

Marshmallows plump on a snowman's hat,
If he comes to life, we'll all have a chat.
Sugar sprinkles dance in the soft winter light,
With each merry bite, everything feels right.

Glimmers of Sugar and Light

Bright lights are twinkling, the cookies are done,
A race to the counter, let the tasting run!
Chocolate chip treasures, who could resist?
The smell is so good, it's hard to desist.

With each little nibble, a giggle, a smile,
Sugar rush dances go on for a while.
Grandma's secret recipes, every last bite,
We bask in the sweetness, pure holiday light.

Sweet Twists and Warm Glows

Candy canes dance in the breeze,
Chasing gumdrops, as sweet as cheese.
Chocolate rivers flow, oh so bright,
In a candy land, everything's right.

Lollipops sing while they sway,
Jellybeans tumble, join the play.
Marshmallow clouds in a cotton sky,
Giggling giggles as we fly high.

Gummy bears hug in sweet delight,
Caramel drizzles, oh what a sight!
Cookies crumble with a cheery shout,
In this land, there's never a doubt.

Frosting rivers and cookie dough hills,
Bouncing along with plenty of thrills.
Every twist brings a smile, oh my!
In Sweet Twists, we'll never say bye!

Sugar Stripes in Twilight

Sunset drapes the lollipops bright,
Candy stripes blossom in twilight.
Cotton candy clouds puff up high,
As our giggles fill the soft sky.

Tootsie rolls roll, a fun surprise,
Underneath the licorice skies.
Chocolate chips twinkle like stars,
Banana peels drive cookie cars.

Bouncing bubbles of grape soda pop,
Chasing the sweetness, we never stop.
Gummy worms wiggle, dancing free,
In the twilight, just you and me.

Sugar-coated dreams, they ignite,
Under the glow of candy light.
In this jolly candy parade,
Sugar stripes, our worries allayed.

A Flicker of Festive Whimsy

Twinkle lights on a gingerbread house,
Frosted windows hide a sneakouse.
Elves in the yard play games galore,
Kicking around candy, who could ask for more?

Marshmallow snowfalls from cake-shaped skies,
With sprinkles and laughter, no room for sighs.
Winking candles with glee on the cake,
Wishing for fun, make no mistake.

Gumdrops scatter with a pop and a cheer,
Jovial songs fill the festive sphere.
Tinsel reflections dance in delight,
At this whimsical fest, everything's right.

Bouncing with joy, we shimmy and sway,
Sipping on cocoa, let's play all day!
With hugs made of frosting, we twirl like a breeze,
In flickers of whimsy, we're bound to please!

Gleaming Sweets and Soft Shadows

Chocolate fountains gleam with delight,
Dancing under soft shadows at night.
Cupcakes twirl in a sugary swirl,
As dreamers around them, we happily twirl.

Marzipan moons rise up in the sky,
Jellybeans bounce and oh, how they fly!
Oh, the sweetness wraps us in joy,
With every bite, we feel like a toy.

Whipped cream mountains just begging for taste,
At this sugar fest, there's no need for haste.
With every giggle, more laughter grows,
In the warmth of sweets, that's how it goes.

Gleaming treats and shadows we cast,
In this candy dream, oh what a blast!
Let's nibble on joy with jaws wide apart,
In these sweet moments, we pour out our heart!

Joyful Lights and Edible Magic

Twinkling lights dance on trees,
Gingerbread men with knobbly knees.
Marshmallow snowmen on the lawn,
Even the carrots start to yawn.

Chocolate fountains make a splash,
Candy canes in a colorful stash.
Cupcakes singing with icing glee,
Every bite's a laughing spree.

Luminous Treats on Frosted Eves

On frosted eves with twinkling stars,
Cookies shaped like shiny cars.
Sprinkles fall like cheerful rain,
Frosting rivers, candy trains.

Giggles burst from every plate,
Lollipops that navigate.
Taffy pulls like hugs so tight,
Sweet enchantments, pure delight.

A Cauldron of Warm Colors

In a cauldron, colors blend,
Laughing pumpkins, what a trend!
Hot cocoa bubbles, marshmallow fluff,
Sipping joy, can't get enough.

Green and orange, swirl and spin,
Cinnamon sticks, let the fun begin.
Magic brews with every taste,
Found with giggles, never waste.

Tidings of Sweetness and Serenity

Peaceful tidings, sweetness all around,
Lemonade rivers where laughter found.
Fruitcake jokes that bounce and jiggle,
Candy laughs that make you giggle.

Serenity sweet, like sugar's kiss,
Life's little moments, nothing amiss.
Joyful hearts, together they sing,
In the season of sweets, happiness is king.

Hues of Hope and Sweet Embrace

In a world so bright and bold,
Colors of hope dare to unfold.
Each hue a dream, a laugh, a cheer,
Sprinkles of joy, we hold so dear.

With candy skies and gummy bears,
We dance on clouds, forget our cares.
A touch of sweetness, oh so grand,
With every hug, a treat in hand.

So paint your life in vibrant shades,
Let laughter shine, let worries fade.
In every corner, joy can trace,
The colors of hope and sweet embrace.

Embrace the quirks, the silly fun,
Life's a game, we've just begun.
With every giggle, let's ignite
The hues of hope and sheer delight!

The Luminance of Seasonal Delights

Seasons change, oh what a sight,
With pumpkins bright, and snowbirds' flight.
Crisp autumn leaves in rusted hues,
And summer nights with starry views.

In winter's grasp, we cozy up,
With cocoa warm inside our cup.
Spring's flowers bloom, a bright parade,
As summer sun makes fireflies fade.

Oh, how the flavors twist and twirl,
Cinnamon swirls and minty whirl.
With each season's taste, let's celebrate,
A feast of joy that's truly great!

So raise a toast, let laughter ring,
To every season and delight it brings.
In each bite and sip, a blissful flight,
The luminance of every seasonal bite!

An Enchantment of Flame and Flavor

In a kitchen bubbling with delight,
Magic brews both day and night.
Sprinkles of spice, a dash of cheer,
Flavors enchanting—food's a seer.

With sizzling pans and cracking eggs,
We toast to life on happy dregs.
Grill marks dance on burgers fair,
Taste buds jive in smoky air.

A pot of dreams, so rich and warm,
Each flavor twist, a playful charm.
With laughter shared, a tasty plot,
An enchantment lived in every pot.

So grab a fork and join the throng,
In this banquet where we belong.
With flames that flicker, flavors in stream,
Life's a feast, so let's all dream!

Glistening Treats in Hushed Moments

In quiet corners, glistening sweets,
Whispers of chocolate, delightful feats.
The crunch of a biscuit, a jellybean's cheer,
In hushed moments, treats appear.

A sprinkle of sugar, a drizzle of fun,
Silent joy when all's said and done.
With every nibble, joy takes flight,
Glistening treats in the soft moonlight.

Hide some candies in shadows deep,
A treasure hunt where secrets sleep.
Laughter echoes, as friends unite,
In the glow of treats, we feel so light.

So savor the silence, the sweet delight,
In glistening moments, all feels right.
A bite of magic, soft and slow,
In every hush, let the sweetness flow!

Tinsel and Sugary Traces

Tinsel on the tree, so bright,
Hiding gumdrops out of sight.
Cats in sweaters, quite a sight,
Chasing candy with delight.

Cookies stacked in towers tall,
Frosting drips and splatters all.
Elves are napping, hear the call,
To eat the sweets before the fall!

Neighbors peeking through their blinds,
Merry chaos, too much fun finds.
A gingerbread house that unwinds,
With frosting dogs and jelly minds.

Snowflakes candy-coated lie,
While hot cocoa waves goodbye.
Laughing kids, a sugary pie,
Who knew sweets could make us fly?

A Festive Glow of Sweet Reflections

Lights twinkle on the grounds,
While the aroma of sugar abounds.
People untangle, making sounds,
Of laughter and joy that surrounds.

Marshmallows melting in mugs,
Hugging whipped cream like snug bugs.
Barnyard animals, bear-hugged rugs,
Join in the dance, give each other shrugs.

Pinecones wrapped in ribbons here,
Squirrels toast with mugs of cheer.
Over the laughter, everything's clear,
Even the snowmen share a beer!

Fruitcake jokes, they fill the air,
For every bite, we laugh and share.
Merry mishaps, joys laid bare,
Festive spirits everywhere!

Cheers to Glistening Confections

Lollipop trees stand so grand,
With peppermint paths and gingerbread land.
Frolicking fairies, they play unplanned,
Filling our hearts with joy so grand.

Chocolate rivers flow delight,
With gummy bears soaring in flight.
Candy canes dance with all their might,
Creating giggles as they ignite.

Jolly old man in a jolly sleigh,
Delivers sweets the whimsical way.
With sprinkles flying in glorious sway,
He'll bring cheer and laughter today!

So raise your glasses, toast to the fun,
With cupcakes galore for everyone!
Let's party till the day is done,
In a world where sweets have won!

The Warm Embrace of Sugar and Light

Candles flicker, shadows dance,
As jellybeans join us by chance.
Sugar and spice in sweet romance,
Let's twirl around in this grand expanse.

The cocoa pot sings a warm song,
While cookies bake and laughter flows strong.
Gumdrops cheer, it won't be long,
'Til everyone joins in the throng.

Pine-scented hugs wrap around,
With frosty smiles that abound.
The magic of joy can be found,
In every hug, every sound.

Soers, let's celebrate tonight,
With cakes that sparkle, oh what a sight!
To sugary dreams and pure delight,
May our hearts shine forever bright!

Sweet Whispers Beneath the Stars

The moon's a giant cookie, oh so bright,
It glows and winks like it's out of sight.
We dance with shadows, giggling like fools,
Underneath the stars, breaking all the rules.

A comet races by, and I shout with glee,
'Catch me a slice of that cosmic pastry!'
But you just laugh and throw me a glance,
'No dessert for you, just this silly dance!'

The crickets sing sweetly, a night-time tune,
While frogs croak along, making quite the swoon.
We trade silly secrets, whisper soft and low,
Under starry skies, what a celestial show!

So here's to the night, where dreams take a spin,
With giggles and starlight, let the fun begin.
We'll eat all the giggles and laugh till we're sore,
With sweet whispers of joy, who could ask for more?

The Glow of Happiness in Every Bite

A cupcake sits gleaming, a sugary sun,
It's dressed up in sprinkles, oh, what fun!
I'll take a big bite, and let out a cheer,
The frosting is singing, 'Eat me, my dear!'

Chocolate chips wink from their cozy spot,
Saying, 'You know we're the best, like it or not!'
I'll share with my friends, or I guess I should try,
But crumbs on my chin make me laugh and cry.

Donuts all frosted, like pillows of joy,
Whispering sweet secrets, my new favorite toy.
We munch and we crunch 'til the day's nearly done,
In the glow of happiness, we've all just won!

So raise up your forks, let's toast with our treats,
Here's to all the smiles that make life so sweet!
With each little nibble, here's to our fate,
The glow of happiness is the best kind of great!

Celestial Candies and Soft Ember Light

A twinkling candy shop floats up in the sky,
With lollipops spinning as comets fly by.
The stars are like gummies, colorful, bold,
With wishes as sprinkles, all stories retold.

Moonbeams pour chocolate, melting so slow,
While marshmallow clouds put on quite the show.
We reach for the rainbow, which tastes like delight,
In this land of candy, all worries take flight.

Peanut butter meteors come crashing nearby,
While starfruit explodes, making tastebuds cry!
The soft ember light warms our giggles and grins,
As we chase down the comet, let the fun begin!

So here's to the sweetness, the joy and the cheer,
With celestial candies, our troubles disappear.
Let laughter and sprinkles fly high through the night,
In the cosmic candy shop, everything feels right!

Heartfelt Moments Wrapped in Warmth

A hug made of cookies, warm from the oven,
Each crumb filled with laughter, I'm feeling like lovin'.
We gather together, a kettle of tea,
Sipping sweet moments, just you and me.

Blankets wrapped tightly, like clouds above,
Whispers of friendship, and stories of love.
With smiles painted bright, on everyone's face,
We fill up the room with our joyful embrace.

Board games are waiting, let the fun unfold,
With laughter like fireworks, our hearts never cold.
Each roll of the dice, a memory made,
In heartfelt moments, our worries do fade.

So here's to the warmth, that hot cocoa brings,
With marshmallows bouncing, oh, how my heart sings!
Together, forever, in our little nest,
With heartfelt moments, we're truly blessed!

Infusions of Cheer beneath Winter Stars

Hot cocoa in my cup, oh what a prize,
Marshmallows floating like fluffy white skies.
The snowman wants a hat, but I say 'no',
He looks good just standing in the snow!

The stars above twinkle, they look so bright,
But I'm focused on cookies baked just right.
With sprinkles and frosting, a sugary dream,
I'll eat them all fast—oh, that's my theme!

Harmonies of Frost and Sugar

A cake sprinkled with frost, it sings so sweet,
It dances on the table, oh what a treat!
A bite brings giggles, sugar rush here we go,
Silly faces everywhere, 'my, look at those!'

Frosted windows show winter's chilly side,
But inside we mingle with laughter and pride.
We bake up some cookies that look like a mess,
But that's the best part, I must confess!

A Cuddle of Warmth and Flavor

In a blanket of snuggles, we sip hot tea,
Flavors of ginger make everything free.
The cat steals my spot, oh what a surprise,
He purrs like a heater, much to my demise!

Cookies fresh from the oven, they dance in a line,
They beckon and lure me, oh how they shine!
With bites of sweet chocolate, laughter will flow,
In this cozy kitchen, it's all in the glow.

Candied Radiance Amidst the Glow

Candy canes hanging on the tree so tall,
I'm pondering theft, will I take one after all?
The lights are a twinkle, like stars in the fray,
They flicker and giggle, then lead me astray!

Gingerbread houses, they gleam like no other,
But frosting's a killer when you just want to smother.
A bite here and there, oh, what a delight,
My taste buds are dancing, oh what a night!

Striped Memories Under Starry Nights

Beneath the sky, we danced so free,
With ants in our pants, not just debris.
Our stripes like zebras, we twirled around,
Laughing at shadows, joy unbound.

We climbed the trees, as if they were seas,
In pirate hats made from soggy leaves.
Whispers of laughter rolled like the tide,
In striped pajamas, we held our pride.

Stars winked at us, bright and true,
While we plotted adventures, just a few.
A caper with aliens, what a delight,
Striped memories made on those starry nights.

When morning broke, with sunlight's spark,
We swore to return to our dreaming park.
In our minds, the stripes would brightly gleam,
Forever the fabric of childhood's dream.

Warmth in a Cup of Cheer

A cup of cheer on a chilly day,
With marshmallows floating, blissful display.
Each sip a smile, a hug in disguise,
Warmth in the mug, joy on the rise.

Spilling a little, oh what a mess!
Laughter erupts, it's anyone's guess.
We spill the tea, but keep secrets tight,
Sipping our giggles through the moonlight.

Cinnamon sprinkles dance on the rim,
As we dream of adventures, our faces all grim.
In the cup of cheer, our worries float high,
With each tasty gulp, we can fly.

Frothy concoctions lead us astray,
With every sweet sip, we twist and we play.
So here's to the mugs, full of delight,
Cheers to our laughter that feels just right.

Threading Dreams and Festive Gleam

Threading dreams on a silver string,
Dancing like elves, hearts full of spring.
Decorated with wishes, bright and bold,
Glimmers of joy in stories retold.

Tinsel and glitter, a sparkly mess,
Our tangled yarn brings a laugh, no stress.
Strumming on strings, with glee we sing,
A chorus of mischief our laughter brings.

Lights all aglow, like fireflies choose,
To float beside us, ignite and amuse.
Creating a canvas where memories beam,
Threading our lives like a whimsical dream.

In this festive dance, let's paint the night,
With colors of giggles, pure and bright.
Through laughter we'll weave, what a sweet team,
Together in joy, we fulfill our dream.

A Sweet Embrace in Flickering Glow

In flickering glow, we find our spark,
With chocolate fondue and laughter in the dark.
Marshmallows toast on a buttery flame,
A sweet embrace, life's not just a game.

With friends all around and stories to share,
Each burst of giggles hangs thick in the air.
S'mores in our hands, too sticky to hold,
Yet joy is the treasure, far more than gold.

A campfire flickers, shadows dance near,
We roast our dreams with a cup of cheer.
Each flicker a memory, bright and bold,
Wrapped in the warmth, our stories unfold.

So here's to the night, and hugs all around,
With sugary smiles, true magic is found.
In every sweet moment, let laughter bestow,
A sweet embrace in the flickering glow.

Peppermint Echoes of the Hearth

In the kitchen, cookies dance,
Sugar rush, in a merry trance.
Flour fights and doughball fights,
Sprinkles fly into moonlit nights.

Grandma's voice, the holiday cheer,
Whispers sweetly, drawing near.
Her secret recipe, just a tease,
In the oven, smells of cheese.

The cat, he spies the gingerbread,
Paws at risk, a life of dread.
He pounces high, but takes a dive,
Now we laugh, he's hardly alive.

Gifts are wrapped with ribbons tight,
Mom's wild art, quite a sight!
Underneath the tree they gleam,
"Will it open?!" Everyone screams!

Glimmering Treats and Cozy Corners

Hot cocoa swirls, marshmallow peaks,
Sipping slow, it's laughter speaks.
Choco stains on chubby cheeks,
We enjoy the quiet weeks.

Baking cupcakes, sprinkles rain,
Flour clouds, what a sweet pain.
Tasting gooey, icing drips,
Covering hands, those yummy grips.

Fireplace crackles, warmth so right,
Squirrels gossip, day turns night.
We gather close, the glow of fun,
Stories shared 'til day is done.

Tinsel tangled, lights askew,
Who can fix this? Guess it's you!
In the chaos, joy we find,
Making memories, sweet and kind.

Twinkling Lollipop Nights

Stars are winking, candy canes,
Frolicking on sugar trains.
Lollipops like twinkling stars,
Candy dreams, oh the bizarre!

Children giggle, laughter bright,
Chasing shadows in the night.
Hiding behind the great big tree,
Planning mischief, wild and free.

Marshmallow snowmen stand so proud,
Waving hello to every crowd.
With gumdrop eyes, they surely smile,
While we munch for quite a while.

Giggles bubble as we meet,
Just two friends on a sugar street.
Hand in hand, with hearts so light,
Dancing under twinkling lights.

Holiday Hues and Gentle Flames

Hues of red and green abound,
Every corner, joy is found.
Wreaths that sparkle, bows that jive,
Bursting colors come alive.

Candles flicker, shadows sway,
Whisper secrets, night and day.
The scent of cinnamon in the air,
Merry moments everywhere.

Mistletoe hangs, a lover's trap,
One swift kiss, then a laugh, a clap.
A dog jumps in, thinks it's a game,
Rushing in, "You're all to blame!"

With every cheer and every giggle,
Happiness makes our hearts wiggle.
So let us toast with cups raised high,
To laughter, love—our favorite pie!

Calmness in Confections and Flame

In a world of chocolate and marshmallow clouds,
I find my zen in fudgey shrouds.
With every bite, my worries fade,
As candy dreams begin to cascade.

Cotton candy spun with care,
Whirls of sweetness hanging in the air.
Lollipop licks soothe my soul,
In this sugary sanctuary, I am whole.

Gumdrops giggle, jellybeans leap,
The laughter of sweets, a joy to keep.
As caramel rivers flow through my mind,
In this land of candy, peace I find.

So light the flames of my candy spree,
As I toast to flavors, wild and free.
With sugar-powered calmness, I declare,
In confections, my worries vanish, I swear.

The Symphony of Sugar and Spark

In a world where sweets play the tune,
Sugar strings hum under the moon.
A marshmallow orchestra begins to sway,
While chocolate flutes dance night away.

Candy canes march in sparkling rows,
Drizzled with laughter, the sweetness flows.
Meringue trumpets blast a sugary sound,
In this symphony, joy is found.

The licorice bass provides a fun beat,
As jellybean dancers twirl on their feet.
Cupcakes with frosting join in the mix,
Creating a spectacle of candy tricks.

So let's all gather for this delight,
With confectionery music well into the night.
Each treat bears a sparkle, a laugh, and a song,
In the symphony of sugar, where we all belong.

Night's Embrace in Peppermint Hues

The moon's a peppermint, shining so bright,
In a world filled with candy, oh what a sight!
Licorice shadows dance with glee,
Under minty stars, so wild and free.

Chocolate whispers to the lurking night,
While gumdrops giggle in pure delight.
Fudgey dreams take flight and spin,
As sweetened breezes blow from within.

Sugar plums waltz with marzipan beams,
Creating a canvas of candy dreams.
Licorice skies, so dark and deep,
Invite us to indulge, while the world's asleep.

So let's celebrate the night's flavored grace,
In peppermint hues, we find our place.
As candy kisses drift from above,
In night's embrace, we're wrapped in love.

Dances in the Glow of Festive Sweetness

In a gingerbread hall, we gather around,
With a flurry of sweets, our joys abound.
Dancing on frosting, we twirl with cheer,
As the spirit of sweetness draws us near.

Lemon drops spin in jubilant glee,
While raspberry ribbon does a jig by the tree.
Sundae frolics and brownie hops,
In this festival of flavors, the fun never stops.

Sparkling skittles light up the floor,
As peppermint patty partners explore.
With every step, sugar sprinkles shine,
Creating a rhythm that's oh-so divine.

So grab your friends and join the spree,
In this glowing dance of sugary glee.
With festive sweetness, our hearts ignite,
As we twirl through the magic of the night.

Bright Shadows in a Winter's Haven

In the snow, a rabbit hops,
Chasing shadows, round and tops.
But when it slips, what a sight,
Wiggling its tail, oh what a fright!

Snowmen grin with carrot noses,
Wearing hats made from old roses.
A snowball fight breaks out in glee,
But the dog thinks it's a game for he!

Hot cocoa spills from cups so wide,
Melting marshmallows that can't hide.
The cat jumps up, pawing foam,
Wondering why it can't take home.

Winter nights with a warm, bright glow,
Sipping tea while the cold winds blow.
Laughter fills the chilly air,
As snowflakes swirl without a care.

Twinkling Lollipops in the Dark

In the night, stars twinkling high,
Lollipops spinning, oh my my!
Candy canes lean to whisper sweet,
While gumdrops dance on their little feet.

The moon's a peach in a cake so round,
While jellybeans bounce off the ground.
A chocolate river flows through the town,
Where gummy bears jump up and down!

Cotton candy clouds float afar,
Each one holding a candy star.
Candy wrappers crinkle and sing,
As all the sweets take to the wing.

In this land of sugary delight,
It's a carnival each starry night.
With every bite, a giggle's sparked,
In the world of lollipops in the dark.

Hearthside Dreams and Sweet Wishes

By the fire, where the shadows flicker,
A wish upon a log, it grows bigger.
Marshmallows roast, toasty and warm,
While silly socks cling to the charm.

Tales of elves with pointy shoes,
And giggling fairies with dancing blues.
A cat curled tight, dreaming of fish,
While kids whisper softly, casting their wish.

A flicker of dreams flows like a stream,
Hearthside laughter turns playful and beam.
With each curl of smoke that takes flight,
They wish for a world so cozy tonight!

The night stretches long, filled with cheer,
With cookies and tales that tickle the ear.
Hearthside warmth keeps troubles far,
In dreams of sweet wishes, we shine like a star.

Flickers of Joy in a Winter Wonderland

Snowflakes twirl with a giggle and spin,
As children laugh, trying to win.
A sled race down a hill so steep,
"Last one down is a snowman's sheep!"

Fluffy scarves wrapped around in knots,
Hats perched high, collecting spots.
The frost paints trees with frosty lace,
While snowmen strike a funny face.

Hot soup bubbles with a whimsical cheer,
As everyone gathers, drawing near.
Biting into cookies, chocolate whole,
The taste ignites a warm, happy soul.

Candles flicker as the night draws close,
While sweet dreams dance, everyone knows.
In this winter land, so bright and free,
Flickers of joy make us all agree!

Embracing Frosty Delights and Flickers

Snowflakes dance like tiny ghosts,
While I sip cocoa, toast to toasts.
Frosty air fills my lungs, oh dear!
Hot chocolate spills—my biggest fear!

The snowman smiles, his nose awry,
A carrot thief who's up to sly.
He wobbles, giggles, what a sight,
In a winter world, full of light!

Lights twinkle bright on the trees,
Hoping they won't attract the bees.
As icicles dangle, I dare a lick,
Nature's ice pop—oh, so slick!

With marshmallows frolicking around,
Every sip is joyfully profound.
Embracing treats, both frosty and sweet,
In winter's embrace, life is a feat!

Tasting the Glow of the Season

Candles flicker like fireflies,
As I gorge on pie that defies.
Pumpkin spice in my latte blend,
With every sip, my heart does mend.

Gingerbread men run from the plate,
Shouting, 'Catch us! We're getting late!'
Sugar cookies beg for a bite,
Sweetness glows in soft moonlight.

Mistletoe hangs, and I'm caught here,
With an awkward kiss, oh dear, oh dear!
Sipping cider, I turn a shade,
Funny moments I wouldn't trade.

In this season of laughter and glee,
Sugarplums dance, wild and free.
Tasting joy, with every cheer,
Let's raise a glass to winter's beer!

Sweets Beneath the Whispering Pines

Under pines, where whispers swirl,
Sweets abound, oh what a whirl!
Brownies hide in cozy nooks,
While fudge sits, grinning in the books.

Candy canes, a forest of red,
Dreamy thoughts dance in my head.
Gumdrops sparking like bright gems,
Who needs diamonds or diadems?

Marshmallow moons float in the sky,
Toasting them makes the sugar fly.
S'mores are calling, so let's explore,
With chocolate oozing, I want more!

Beneath these whispering pines so grand,
Sweets and laughter go hand in hand.
A candy feast, what a sweet sight,
In nature's joy, our hearts take flight!

The Charm of Twisted Flavors

Twisted flavors in a cupcake swirl,
Chocolate, chili—give it a whirl!
Lemon with bacon, what a surprise,
Life's full of wonders that mesmerize.

Pickles in brownies? You think I'm mad?
But take a bite—it's just a fad!
Sour cream frosting, oh so divine,
Taste the crazy—it's all in the design!

Mustard on ice cream? Dare to try!
It's a wild ride that'll make you sigh.
Spicy jalapeño on sweet bread toast,
In the land of odd, I'm the host!

So let's embrace the weird and fun,
In the kitchen, we've just begun.
With every flavor, every twist,
Who knew being quirky could feel like bliss?

The Soft Glow of Seasonal Treats

A cookie here, a brownie there,
The frosting floofs, they swing with flair.
With sprinkles raining down like snow,
I'll eat them all, just watch me go!

The pie sits cool upon the rack,
But I won't wait, I've lost my knack.
A slice or two, oh what a feat,
I'll eat and dance with ginger feet!

The cake that glistens, oh so bright,
I might just tackle it tonight.
With whipped cream mountains piled real high,
I'll swim in sweetness, oh me, oh my!

In every bite there's joy and glee,
The pumpkin bread is calling me.
With coffee strong, we'll laugh and cheer,
The soft glow of treats, oh my dear!

Bright Stripes Against the Frost

Oh stripes of red, and stripes of green,
My fashion choice might seem unseen.
I twirl around with flair and fun,
Stripes against frost, I've surely won!

With mittens bright, and hats so tall,
I stumble, trip, and sometimes fall.
These stripes, they help me blend right in,
The snowball fight, let's all begin!

But who's to say what's winter wear?
An elf-like outfit gives a scare!
With jingle bells all wrapped around,
I strut my stripes, I own this town!

So if you see me at the mall,
Just know, my stripes are there to brawl.
Against the frost, I'll make my way,
With laughter bright, I'll seize the day!

A Cheerful Glow in Chill's Embrace

A cup of cocoa warms my hands,
In winter's chill, I make my plans.
With marshmallows that bob and dance,
I take a slurp, oh what a chance!

The snowflakes swirl like cheeky sprites,
They tickle noses in wintry nights.
With cheeky grins, we laugh and play,
In cozy corners, we'll laugh away!

Scarves wrapped tight, we bound about,
In snowball fights, there's no room for doubt.
My cheeks are rosy, a lovely sight,
In chill's embrace, we shine so bright!

So let the weather do its worst,
With hot cocoa and fun, I'll quench my thirst.
Through every snowstorm, let's not fret,
A cheerful glow, no need to sweat!

Festive Whirls and Shining Nights

The twinkle lights are strung with care,
They shine so bright, they fill the air.
With every turn, my skirt does swirl,
In festive whirls, I give a twirl!

The snowman wears a jaunty hat,
He's got a carrot and looks quite fat.
We give him friends and watch him grin,
A holiday sight, let's now begin!

The cookies baked with sugar glows,
In dancing dreams, my laughter flows.
With peppermint sticks that taste like cheer,
Let's party hard, this time of year!

So raise a toast with mugs so high,
To festive nights that make us sigh.
In whirls of joy, we dance about,
Shining nights, there's never doubt!

The Magic of Holiday Sweets

In the kitchen, pots do clatter,
Cookies rise, nobody gets fatter.
Candy canes hanging from trees,
Sweet aromas carried on the breeze.

Sprinkles fly with joyous glee,
Frosting battles, you can't flee.
Gingerbread men doing a jig,
One small bite, oh, that was big!

Marshmallows dance in a cocoa sea,
Whipped cream waves, won't let it be.
Choc-o-lot! A cake so keen,
I almost lost my ice cream bean.

On this holiday, don't fear the sweets,
It's all in fun, no need for feats.
So grab a treat, let laughter spill,
In the land of sugar, find your thrill!

Whirls of Color in Winter's Glow

Winter's colors start to swirl,
Snowflakes dance, as if they twirl.
Red-nosed reindeer in a race,
Racing round at an unusual pace.

Hot cocoa spills all over me,
Who knew mugs could be so free?
The snowman winks with a carrot nose,
While snowballs fly, as friendship grows.

Sleds go zoom down hills so steep,
Kids laugh hard, but then they weep.
A snowy face but that's all right,
As long as it's fun, we'll hold on tight!

Colors burst in the winter's night,
The holiday lights shine so bright.
So grab your coat, don't be too slow,
Join in the fun of winter's glow!

A Dance of Light and Flavor

Dancing in the kitchen, pots a-jive,
Each ingredient feels alive.
Butter flips and flour flies,
In this chef world, I'm quite the prize!

Sautéed veggies wear a fancy hat,
While pasta spins like a playful cat.
Pizza slices take a bow,
As cheese does melt – oh, holy cow!

Candies hop around with cheer,
Lollipops shout, "We're glad you're here!"
Chocolate fountains flow like streams,
Creating bubbles of creamy dreams.

With every bite, a spark ignites,
In this dance of flavors, everything's right.
So twirl with joy, let laughter soar,
As we feast our hearts for evermore!

Sugary Camels and Gentle Light

In desert dunes, camels roam,
With sweet treats to make them feel at home.
Candy dates and honey drips,
They navigate with sugary trips.

Underneath the twinkling stars,
They share tales of candy bars.
With a sprinkle here, and a gummy there,
Their laughter travels through the air.

Gentle light shines from above,
Camels sway with the taste of love.
Lemon drops and caramel bites,
A treat parade on magical nights.

So join the camels, don't be shy,
In this land of sweets, we'll fly high.
With every giggle, joy ignites,
Together we'll savor sweet delights!

Sweet Dreams Under Stardust

As I lay on my bed of fluff,
I dream of unicorns and stuff.
With candy clouds and gumdrop rain,
I wake up hoping it's not in vain.

The moon's a cookie, crisp and tight,
I nibble stars to end the night.
A sprinkle fairy dances slow,
She tells me secrets only I know.

Lollipop trees in a candy land,
Where marshmallow critters play on sand.
I chase them round, they giggle loud,
Echoes of sweetness in a fluffy cloud.

When dawn peeks in with sleepy eyes,
I rush to taste the morning skies.
With breakfast donuts far and wide,
Each bite's a dream I won't abide.

Reflecting Warm Stories and Sugary Wishes

In the glow of the butter lamp,
I tell my tales as shadows cramp.
With syrup rivers a-flowing bright,
Dreams tumble out just like a kite.

Each story sizzles, caramel twist,
Chocolates jump and dance, insist.
With gummies giggling all around,
Sweet whispers echo, love is found.

A bear in pajamas joins our chat,
Wearing a hat, just look at that!
We share a smoothie filled with cheer,
Pouring all our wishes, very near.

S'mores in hand, we toast our dreams,
Life is sweeter than it seems.
With every hug, a sprinkle gleams,
Together we weave our sugary themes.

Toasts of Sugars and Flames

Raise a glass of fizzy brew,
Sharing laughs, just me and you.
With cookies to toast this crazy night,
Let's sprinkle some cheer, hold on tight.

The fire crackles, marshmallows roast,
We munch on chocolate, that's our boast.
Each bite's a giggle, each sip's a cheer,
In this sugary blaze, we have no fear.

Let the cupcakes dance in frosted bliss,
With whipped cream hats, it's hard to miss.
We'll jive to the tune of candy canes,
In this sweet circus, nothing contains.

So here's to us, in frothy glee,
With laughter loud, as sweet as can be.
In every toast, a sugary spark,
Together we'll shine through the dark.

Whispers of Delight in the Dark

The night is thick, but giggles blend,
As candy critters come to lend.
With whispers soft that twirl and spin,
They seek the treasures found within.

A chocolate rover sprinkles cheer,
While gumball dreams bounce, that's quite near.
In the quiet, a marshmallow sighs,
As we share secrets, under starlit skies.

Licorice paths lead us away,
Where jellybeans dance and frolic play.
In this dark, sweet wonders unfold,
Today's plain tale is tomorrow's gold.

Let's mend our hearts with sweet delights,
And lull the world with sugary sights.
In shadows deep, our joy ignites,
With whispers of glee on magical nights.

Warmth Found in Rituals of Light

Candles flicker, dance and sway,
They threaten to melt my cheese today.
I assure them it's not a crime,
To have a snack while passing time.

The glow of bulbs in colorful rows,
Reminds me how to find my toes.
I trip on cords, I laugh and shout,
How did I lose the lights about?

With every spark, my heart takes flight,
Then promptly lands on the puppy's bite.
Warmth of love, a toasty sight,
Ignites a cheer, with little fright.

Oh ritual of warmth, oh glow of cheer,
You keep us smiling, year after year.
Just mind the cat, in all her grace,
She'll take the treats, then clear the space.

Blushing Lights in a Winter's Embrace

Winter's chill gives quite the tease,
I smile at lights wrapped around the trees.
They blink like eyes, winking with glee,
To tease the frost, just wait and see.

Snowflakes fall, they're all around,
Hot cocoa spills, that's the sound.
Marshmallows bounce, they float with pride,
I'll need a sled to get outside.

Blushing lights, twinkling bright,
Remind me I wore red last night.
The fridge keeps groaning, it's no surprise,
Leftover pie in my 'no-fall' pies.

Let's gather 'round, sing songs so fine,
While plotting mischief with spiced red wine.
In every laugh, in every cheer,
Warm drinks and hugs through winter's fear.

Echoes of Sweetness in the Night

The moon reflects on icing light,
Cookies waiting, oh what a sight!
I nibble one, just to be fair,
But there's ten more, if you dare.

Whispers of sugar fill the air,
I look around, check if you care.
A mountain of sprinkles, oh so bright,
Inviting dreams float out in flight.

Baking joys, the mixing bowl's fate,
I drop the whisk—where's the plate?
Sweet echoes bounce, knocking at dusk,
With frosting fingers, I feel quite brusque.

Nighttime snacks, oh what a thrill,
Don't mind the crumbs, they're part of the skill.
Catch the giggles, the small delight,
In every bite, oh what a night!

Starry Nights and Sugary Hues

Stars sprinkle sugar across the dark,
Each one winks like a friendly shark.
They giggle softly, share their dreams,
As I attempt to catch their beams.

The skies are painted with sweet delight,
Chocolate rivers, a tasty flight.
I leap and bound, through clouds of cream,
In my mind, I'm a sugary dream.

Cotton candy, a fluffy mess,
I wear it well, I must confess.
Every bite's a little delight,
Stars rumble with laughter, oh what a sight!

With every gleam, my heart takes flight,
In starry nights, filled with pure light.
I tiptoe on sweetness, chasing hues,
In the galaxy where sugar ensues.

Shadows of Sugar and Celebration

In the corner, cookies hide,
With frosting smiles, how they bide.
They sneak away at midnight's toll,
Plotting sweets like a heist of coal.

The cake stands tall, but quakes in fright,
As I approach with fork in sight.
It trembles like it knows my quest,
To conquer all and pass the test.

Chocolate rivers, don't you flow,
Or I might lose my grip, you know!
With sprinkles dancing, oh so bright,
My diet's down, let's take flight!

So raise a glass, and cheer this day,
For sugar's power leads astray.
In shadows deep, let's make a scene,
Where calories cease, and dreams are keen.

Tasting the Night's Sweet Warmth

Beneath the stars, a pie awaits,
It winks at me through cherry gates.
With every slice, a giggle flows,
As whipped cream clouds above it grows.

I nibble on a chocolate moon,
A creamy dream that ends too soon.
The coffee whispers, 'Just one more,'
But I'm already on dessert's floor.

Marshmallows fluff up in surprise,
While brownies wink with cheeky eyes.
A sticky mess, oh what a sight,
I dance with crumbs all through the night.

So hold your spoon and take a chance,
For sugar's spark ignites the dance.
Let's toast with sweets here in delight,
And taste the joys of every bite.

Illuminated Sweets in the Silence

Covered in darkness, the candies gleam,
Like stars that fell from a dentist's dream.
Lollipops glow like lanterns bright,
Leading me on in the quiet night.

Licorice twirls in a graceful prance,
Inviting me for a sugar dance.
With every step, I feel the rush,
Of gummy bears in a juicy hush.

Taffy whispers tales of wonder,
While bubblegum pops like distant thunder.
In this sweetness, I find my peace,
As sugar's hold does never cease.

So let's rejoice in this tender glow,
For sweets illuminate the path I know.
In the silence, let laughter flow,
As we savor treats blow by blow.

The Allure of Glistening Treats

Oh, the cupcakes with their shiny glaze,
They pull me in with dazzling ways.
Each sprinkle's charm, a siren's song,
In this land of sugar, I belong.

The donuts shine like little suns,
Twirling jelly, every bite runs.
With every pop, a taste divine,
These glistening treats, oh, how they shine!

The ice cream parlor beckons me,
With scoops that laugh so joyfully.
A whipped cream mountain! Dive right in,
With cherries on top, let the feast begin!

Let's revel in this sugary quest,
Forget the fridge, we'll never rest.
For every glisten holds a story,
In the world of sweets, there's all the glory!

Winter's Confectionery Embrace

In winter's chill, we find our stash,
A cupboard full of sweets, oh what a bash!
Marshmallows plump, like tiny clouds,
Hot cocoa dreams, we speak them loud.

Frosty bites of caramel are divine,
Candy canes line up, oh how they shine!
Gingerbread men do a funny dance,
Nibbling on cookies, why not take a chance?

Sweater weather with a jellybean twist,
Snowball fights that you can't resist.
With sugary hugs and frosty cheer,
We laugh and munch as winter draws near.

Biting into fudge, it's quite a delight,
Chasing the snowflakes, oh what a sight!
This confectionery embrace is a treat,
Winter, oh winter, you can't be beat!

Gleaming Sticks of Joy

Oh, what's that glimmering in the snow?
A stick of delight—let's see how it goes!
Caramel and chocolate, a gleeful retreat,
Lick it, don't stick it, a sticky-sweet feat.

They shine like stars, with wrappers aglow,
Each bite is a giggle, what a fine show!
But careful, my friends, it's quite a parade,
Gleaming sticks of joy, you won't be dismayed!

When winter gets cold, it's warmth that we crave,
With popsicles hidden that we mistakenly save.
Snowmen munch on marshmallow hats,
While squirrels sip cocoa, wearing their spats!

Laughter erupts with each sugary bite,
Nutty crunches keep spirits so bright.
In winter's embrace, let's dance and enjoy,
With gleaming sticks of joy, oh boy, oh boy!

Illuminated Delights in December

Lights twinkle like stars on a crisp winter night,
Illuminated delights, what a dazzling sight!
Gingerbread houses all decked with flair,
Frosted with laughter and sweets everywhere.

December's a canvas for treats so divine,
Sugar plum visions, oh how they align!
Fuzzy socks cozy, and eggnogs abound,
Wrapped up in giggles, joy is profound.

Festive pies bubbling, scents in the air,
Chocolate fountains—who's brave enough to dare?
Candied fruit cakes that shake and they dance,
Spreading the cheer, let's give it a chance!

With carols that echo and friends gathered near,
Every moment's a spark, share the holiday cheer.
In this season of joy, let's jump, spin, and play,
Illuminated delights make the cold slip away!

Circles of Warmth and Wonder

Gather 'round friends for a tale to be spun,
Circles of warmth, where laughter is fun.
Hot soup and stories, they flow like the breeze,
Sipping on joy while we tease and we squeeze.

The fire crackles softly, our cheeks are aglow,
Sip that cocoa, let the giggles flow!
Snowball battles turn into fits of delight,
With circles of wonder, we dance through the night.

Fluffy slippers and fuzzy hats,
Comfy blankets with pillows and chats.
Each face tells a story, each smile brings cheer,
In these merry circles, winter's dreams are clear.

So grab a friend and join in the spree,
Circles of warmth really bring out glee.
As snowflakes swirl down in a magical way,
We cherish these moments, let's dance and play!

Milton Keynes UK
Ingram Content Group UK Ltd.
UKHW030945071224
452128UK00010B/369